# HO HO HO!

*Riddles about Santa Claus*

by Rick and Ann Walton
pictures by Susan Slattery Burke

## ◣ Lerner Publications Company · Minneapolis

*To Bonnie, who's tops in our Pole*   —R.W. & A.W.

*To my wonderful daughter, Shea, for her incredible inspiration in this first year of her life*   —S.S.B.

Copyright © 1991 by Lerner Publications Company

*This book is available in two editions:*
Library binding by Lerner Publications Company
Soft cover by First Avenue Editions
241 First Avenue North
Minneapolis, MN 55401

Library of Congress Cataloging-in-Publication Data

Walton, Rick
   Ho ho ho!: riddles about Santa Claus/by Rick & Ann Walton; pictures by Susan Slattery Burke.
      p.     cm.
   Summary: A collection of riddles about Santa Claus.
   ISBN 0-8225-2337-X (lib. bdg.)
   ISBN 0-8225-9595-8 (pbk.)
   1. Riddles, Juvenile. 2. Santa Claus—United States—Juvenile humor. [1. Riddles. 2. Santa Claus—Wit and humor.] I. Walton, Ann, 1963-     . II. Burke, Susan Slattery, ill. III. Title.
PN6371.5.W354   1991        818'.5402—dc20        90-28541
                                                  CIP
Manufactured in the United States of America        AC

1  2  3  4  5  6  7  8  9  10  00  99  98  97  96  95  94  93  92  91

**Q:** Why won't Santa give you five cents?

**A:** Because he's Nickle-less.

**Q:** Which reindeer knows Morse code?
**A:** Dasher.

**Q:** How does Santa talk to his reindeer?
**A:** He uses an inter-Com-et.

**Q:** If Santa Claus has twelve reindeer and takes all but three with him on his midnight ride, how many reindeer stay behind?
**A:** Three.

**Q:** Who protects Santa from toy thieves?
**A:** The North Police.

**Q:** What do you get when you cross St. Nicholas with a bear?

**A:** Santa Claws.

**Q:** What's big and brown and lives at the North Pole?

**A:** A lost gorilla.

**Q:** Who takes presents to young crows?

**A:** Santa Caws.

**Q:** Who brings presents to baby sand crabs?

**A:** Sandy Claws.

**Q:** What kind of knot does Santa use to tie up his reindeer?

**A:** A rein-bow knot.

**Q:** Which reindeer is a ball of fire?

**A:** Comet.

**Q:** What do reindeer do when polar bears chase them?

**A:** They run for deer life.

**Q:** What's fast and red and goes, "Oh, oh, oh!"

**A:** Santa Claus flying backwards.

**Q:** What goes, "Ho, ho, ho, OOPS!"

**A:** Santa Claus falling out of his sleigh.

**Q:** Who wears a red cap, bounds across Africa, and gives presents to other animals?

**A:** Santelope.

**Q:** What's black and white and red all over?
**A:** Santa Claus riding a zebra.

**Q:** Who is covered with feathers, lays eggs, and helps pull Santa's sleigh on Christmas Eve?
**A:** Rudolph the Red-Nosed Rein Duck.

**Q:** What's gray, weighs over 10,000 pounds, and comes down your chimney on Christmas Eve?
**A:** A noel-ephant.

**Q:** How do you find Santa?
**A:** Follow the Santa Clues.

**Q:** What does Santa do when he gets soot on his clothes?

**A:** He puts the clothes in his sootcase.

**Q:** Who introduced Santa Claus to Mrs. Claus?

**A:** Cupid.

**Q:** What did Santa give Mrs. Claus for Christmas?

**A:** A Saint Nicklace.

**Q:** What does Santa Claus wear when he dresses up?

**A:** A Nicktie.

**Q:** What does Santa wear all year long?

**A:** Santa Clothes.

**Q:** Where does he keep his Santa Clothes?

**A:** In his Santa Closet.

**Q:** How did Dancer get his name?

**A:** When he met Santa Claus, he said, "My name is Daniel, but you can call me Dan, Sir."

**Q:** Why did the wolf eat Santa Claus?

**A:** Because the wolf thought Santa was Little Red Riding Hood's grandfather.

**Q:** Who makes scary movies about Santa Claus?

**A:** Elf-Red Hitchcock.

**Q:** Where does Christmas come before Thanksgiving?

**A:** In the dictionary.

**Q:** If stockings are filled with presents on Christmas Eve, what are they filled with the rest of the year?

**A:** Feet.

**Q:** What do the elves listen to while they work?

**A:** Gift rap music.

**Q**: Who is Santa's favorite singer?
**A**: Elves Presley.

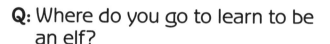

**Q**: Where do you go to learn to be an elf?
**A**: To Santa Class.

**Q**: What's the first thing you learn at Santa Class?
**A**: The elfabet.

**Q**: How do Santa's elves get over the fence into the reindeer pen?
**A**: They do the North Pole Vault.

**Q:** Where does Santa Claus send his elves when they get too noisy?

**A:** To the sh-elf.

**Q:** What do elves like to eat?

**A:** Elfelfa.

**Q:** What did the elves say when the reindeer refused to help make the Christmas goodies?

**A:** "We'll do it ours-elves."

**Q:** Where did Santa Claus grow up?

**A:** In Idaho-ho-ho.

**Q:** Where did Santa learn about holding children on his knee?

**A:** In Lapland.

**Q:** What do Santa Claus's children call him?

**A:** Father Christmas.

**Q:** Is "Saint Nicholas" Santa Claus's real name?

**A:** No, it's his Nick name.

**Q:** If you go to the North Pole, how do you get Santa to let you in his workshop?

**A:** Ring the deerbell.

PLEASE RING

**Q:** Why doesn't Santa think about the past or the future?
**A:** Because he always worries about the present.

**Q:** What do you call the fear of getting stuck in a chimney?
**A:** Santa Claustrophobia.

**Q:** How does Santa know when Christmas is coming?
**A:** He looks at his calen-deer.

**Q:** Why does Santa Claus come down your chimney?

**A:** Because he doesn't have the key to your front door.

**Q:** How does Santa Claus get in your house if you don't have a chimney?

**A:** He finds a ho-ho-hole.

**Q:** Who has red cheeks, a belly that shakes when he laughs like a bowlful of jelly, and climbs down your chimney?

**A:** A fat, jolly chimney sweep with a cold.

**Q:** How does Santa know when it's time to deliver presents?

**A:** He looks at his Santa Clock.

**Q:** How does Santa Claus fit all the presents in his sleigh?

**A:** He puts as much as he can in the front seat, then as much as he can in the back seat, and then he puts the rest in the glove compartment.

**Q:** Where is Santa Claus when the sun goes down on Christmas Eve?

**A:** In the dark.

**Q:** What's the first thing Santa Claus does when he gets in his sleigh?

**A:** He sits down.

**Q:** What do you call a reindeer who does back flips while flying through the air?

**A:** A deerdevil.

**Q:** How did the reindeer know that Santa had fallen out of the sleigh?

**A:** They felt a rein drop.

**Q:** What does Santa do when his reindeer makes a sloppy landing on a housetop?

**A:** He hits the roof.

**Q:** Why doesn't Santa use plastic deer to pull his sleigh?

**A:** Because they're reinproof.

**Q:** Who delivers presents to the moon?
**A:** Claustronauts.

**Q:** How does Santa's sleigh fly in the air?
**A:** Because it uses Santi-gravity.

**Q:** What does Santa ride when he's tired of sleighs and reindeer?
**A:** A ho-ho-horse.

**Q:** When Santa Claus is flying over your town, what does he see on his right hand?
**A:** His mitten.

**Q:** Why does Santa use candles at the North Pole?
**A:** Because where he lives, there's noel-ectricity.

**Q:** What does Santa have on his fireplace mantle?
**A:** Saint Nick-nacks.

**Q:** What's the quickest way to get to the North Pole?
**A:** Take the noel-evator.

**Q:** Where does Santa Claus stay when he's not at the North Pole?

**A:** In ho-ho-ho-tels.

**Q:** Why does Santa Claus carry presents around the world?

**A:** Because the presents won't go by themselves.

**Q:** When does Santa Claus stop flying on Christmas Eve?

**A:** When he lands.

**Q:** Where does Santa Claus go when he's done delivering presents?

**A:** Ho-ho-home.

## ABOUT THE AUTHORS

**Rick and Ann Walton** love to read, travel, play guitar, study foreign languages, and write for children. Rick also collects books and writes music while Ann knits and does origami. They live in Provo, Utah, where Ann is a computer programmer and Rick is planning a military overthrow of the North Pole. They have two outstanding children.

## ABOUT THE ARTIST

**Susan Slattery Burke** loves to illustrate fun-loving characters, especially animals. To her, each of them has a personality all its own. Her satisfaction comes when the characters come to life for the reader as well. Susan lives in Minneapolis, Minnesota, with her husband, her daughter, and their dog and cat. A graduate of the University of Minnesota, Susan enjoys sculpting, travel, illustrating, chasing her daughter, and being outdoors.

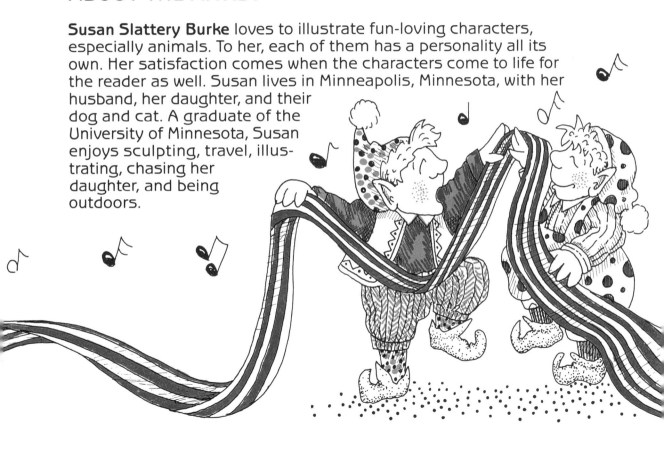

If you like **Ho Ho Ho!**, you'll love
these other **You Must Be Joking** riddle books:

**Alphabatty:** Riddles from A to Z
**Help Wanted:** Riddles about Jobs
**Here's to Ewe:** Riddles about Sheep
**Hide and Shriek:** Riddles about Ghosts and Goblins
**I Toad You So:** Riddles about Frogs and Toads
**On with the Show:** Show Me Riddles
**Out on a Limb:** Riddles about Trees and Plants
**That's for Shore:** Riddles from the Beach
**Weather or Not:** Riddles for Rain and Shine
**What's Gnu?** Riddles from the Zoo
**Wing It!** Riddles about Birds